Let's Write

Flowers, Gardens & Plants

31 Creative Writing Prompts

by Melissa Gijsbers

©2025 Melissa Gijsbers
melissagijsbers.com

Finish This Book Press

Written by Melissa Gijsbers

Cover Design using elements from Canva

ISBN: 978-1-7641755-0-0

All rights reserved. Apart from any permitted use under the Copyright Act, no part of this book may be reproduced, copied, scanned, stored in a retrieval system, recorded or transmitted in any form or by any means, without the prior permission of the publisher.

Dedication

To Renee, who always wears a flower in her hair, and picks up new plants whenever we're at a market

Table of Contents

Dedication iii

Introduction 1

Melissa's Golden Rules of Writing 3

Tips on how to use Writing Prompts 5

Writing Prompts 7

Conclusion 38

About the Author 39

Also by Melissa Gijsbers: 41

Introduction

Welcome writers,

So many people say that to be a writer, you need to write every day. This isn't something I believe. I believe that to be a writer, you need to write. That said, writing every day can be useful as it helps you practice your writing and make progress on whatever you are working on.

One thing that I love to do is play around with writing prompts and see what happens. I get one and write, purely for the joy of writing. Sometimes, these stories turn into something I want to develop into a piece that can be entered in a competition or published, but most of the time, it's simply fun to write. I can let go of any of my worries that I'm not good enough or that not one will enjoy it because I'm simply in the moment and writing for myself.

This is what the *Let's Write* series of books is all about.

Each book contains 31 writing prompts, enough for one a day for a month, with a few extra if you are choosing a month without 31 days. You can also use them at random when you want to write something but don't know where to start.

Each book has a theme, this one is all about flowers, gardens, and plants, and you can use any of the prompts you like and in any way you like. Have fun with them and be creative.

Once you've finished all the prompts in this book, be sure to look out for some of the others in this series or go back and play with them again.

Happy Writing.

Melissa Gijsbers

Melissa's Golden Rules of Writing

1. **Have FUN!** - creative writing is all about the process. After all, if you're not having fun, what's the point?

2. **It's YOUR Story**—write your story your way. There is no single way to write a story, so experiment, play, and write whatever comes to mind.

3. **Experiment**—play with different styles and genre. You never know what you'll enjoy writing until you try. Plus, you don't have to limit yourself to just one type of writing.

4. **Try something new**—if your story isn't working, try something new. A different point of view, style, genre, or even a new prompt if the one you're working on isn't working!

5. **Have FUN!** - Did I mention have fun? Whether you are writing something silly or serious, creating a story is fun, so enjoy it.

6. **Write as long or as short as you like**—If you only have a few minutes, then you can write something short. It doesn't matter if you don't finish a story or piece of writing in a sitting, or at all.

7. **First drafts are meant to be crappy***—this is something many people don't realise, it's no issue if your first draft is not perfect. Everything can be fixed up in the editing process.

8. **You don't have to finish**—if you're writing for fun, and you don't finish your story, that's okay. You can always come back and finish it another time.

9. **Have FUN!** - I may have mentioned this before… have fun writing your story, poem, or whatever else you're writing.

* Crappy = flawed, imperfect, incomplete, not up to scratch, unsatisfactory

Tips on how to use Writing Prompts

1. **Read the prompt carefully**— What is it asking you to do?

2. **Think outside the box**— Is there a way you can use the prompt in a fun or unusual way?

3. **Use the prompt more than once**— If you have more than one idea, then write them down. You can use a prompt in many different ways. You can save them to use next year, or even after Christmas if you get in a story writing mood.

4. **Just write**— Don't worry about titles, spelling, grammar, or anything else, just write. This is a first draft. Underline any words you're not sure about spelling and you can come back to them later. Everything can be fixed up in the editing process.

5. **Read over what you've written**—When you've done, read over what you've written and fix up any obvious errors. Then you can have fun editing your story to share (if you want to).

Writing Prompts

1

Write an ode to your favourite flower or plant

2

Flowers have a special meaning.
Look up the meaning to your favourite flower and use it to inspire a story

3

You are clearing out an overgrown garden and find a flower that you can't identify. Write a story about this new flower

4

Write a story featuring the following flowers: Rose, Peony, Daffodil, Lily, Gerbera

5

Choose a random object. Imagine that object was a plant. Write something featuring that plant

6

In general, people either have a green thumb where they can grow plants, or a black thumb where they can't grow plants.

Write a story about someone with a purple thumb and what that means when it comes to plants

7

You walk past a bouquet of flowers. The flowers start to talk to you.

What do they say? What happens next?

8

Write a story about the person who bought a flower instead of flour by accident!

9

Imagine you wake up one morning to find a huge bean stalk in your back yard.

Write a story about what happens next

10

Write a story about digging a hole

11

There is evidence that playing classical music to plants help them grow.

Write a story where a plant tells you that they don't like classical music and states their surprising musical preference

12

Write a story using this as the last line:

Red roses don't say love to me, only the blue ones do.

13

Imagine you discover a plant that can cure any illness.

Write a story about your discovery

14

Write a story about a bouquet toss at a wedding that doesn't go to plan

15

Write a conversation between two plants

16

Write something featuring a pile of autumn leaves

17

In the middle of the night, you wake up to the sound of a branch knocking on your window.

Write a story about why the tree wanted your attention

18

Write a story about a 100-year-old flower

19

You travel in time and bring back some seeds from a long extinct plant and sow it in your garden.

Write a story about what happens

20

Imagine you are an alien sent to earth to report back about this strange blue and green planet.

Write a report about a tree, flower or other plant

21

You are a spy, dressed up as a tree or bush, to spy on the dullest event imaginable.

Write a story about your evening

22

You are looking in an old book and a pressed flower falls out. You do some research and find out about the owner of the book and the flower.

Write a story about the owner of the book who pressed the flower in its pages

23

Write a story about a child giving a weed flower to someone special

24

Write a story about a wedding, from the point of view of the flower girl

25

Write an obituary for a house plant

26

You move to a new home with an overgrown garden. As you start clearing it out, you discover a secret garden.

Write a story about your discovery

27

Write a story about fairies at the bottom of your garden

28

Write a story about growing the biggest vegetable you can imagine

29

Using the following random words, write a story set in a garden:

car, concrete, orange, house, dragon

30

Write a story about going for a walk through a garden, park, or forest

31

You see a sign in a park saying 'keep off the grass'. Write a story about what happens when you ignore this sign

Conclusion

I hope you've had fun with these writing prompts and enjoyed crafting stories.

One fantastic thing about writing prompts is that you can use them more than once and come out with an entirely different story.

If you do want to use the prompt again and aren't quite sure what to do, try writing from a different point of view, or a different style or genre than you did last time. You can also put this book away for a while and try them all again with a fresh mind.

Try it and see what happens.

If you enjoyed the prompts in this book, be sure to check out the other books in this series as well as my other writing prompt books.

Happy Writing,

Melissa Gijsbers

About the Author

Melissa Gijsbers is an author and booklover. Stories have always been a big part of her life, and she has been writing them for as long as she can remember.

She started working with young writers in 2013 at the Monash Public Library and has been inspiring them to write by providing them with crazy writing prompts ever since! This group helped Melissa discover how important creative writing can be for wellbeing, and how much fun writing prompts can be.

Her first book, *Swallow Me, NOW!* was published in 2014. Since then, she has published more books and written even more stories that may or may not be published.

She currently lives in Gippsland in Victoria, Australia and spends quite a bit of time coming up with fun writing ideas for stories, as well as writing more books herself.

You can find out more about Melissa and her books on her website—www.melissagijsbers.com

Also by Melissa Gijsbers:

Writing Prompt Books

- Genie in my Drink Bottle & other writing prompts
- Great Lost Sock Mystery & other writing prompts
- Writing Prompts – Random Words

Other books

- Swallow Me, NOW!
- 3… 2… 1… Done!
- Lizzy's Dragon
- Lilly's Library
- My Princess Wears a Superhero Cape
- My Mummy is Evil
- Stories Through the Rainbow short story collection
- Creative Writing for Wellbeing
- Active Books for ADHD

www.ingramcontent.com/pod-product-compliance
Lightning Source LLC
Chambersburg PA
CBHW071917070526
44583CB00016B/2034